Words that appear in **bold** type are defined in the glossary on pages 28 and 29.

Please visit our web site at: www.garethstevens.com
For a free color catalog describing Gareth Stevens Publishing's
list of high-quality books and multimedia programs, call
1-800-542-2595 (USA) or 1-800-387-3178 (Canada).
Gareth Stevens Publishing's fax: (414) 332-3567.

Library of Congress Cataloging-in-Publication Data

Baumbusch, Brigitte.
    Food in art / by Brigitte Baumbusch.
        p. cm. — (What makes a masterpiece?)
    Includes index.
    ISBN 0-8368-4380-0 (lib. bdg.)
    1. Food in art—Juvenile literature. I. Title. II. Series.
    N8217.F64B38   2004
    704.9'496413—dc22   2004045382

This edition first published in 2005 by
Gareth Stevens Publishing
A World Almanac Education Group Company
330 West Olive Street, Suite 100
Milwaukee, Wisconsin 53212 USA

Copyright © Andrea Dué s.r.l. 2000

This U.S. edition copyright © 2005 by Gareth Stevens, Inc.
Additional end matter copyright © 2005 by Gareth Stevens, Inc.

Translator: Erika Pauli

Gareth Stevens series editor: Dorothy L. Gibbs
Gareth Stevens art direction: Tammy West

Printed in the United States of America

1 2 3 4 5 6 7 8 9 08 07 06 05 04

FOOD in Art

by Brigitte Baumbusch

GARETH**STEVENS**
GS PUBLISHING
A World Almanac Education Group Company

What makes food . . .

This endless **expanse** of colorful things to eat was painted by a **contemporary** artist from Iceland. His name is Erro, and he calls this painting "Foodscape," in other words, a "**landscape** of food." If you look closely, you will see a **horizon** off in the distance.

a masterpiece?

Some foods have always been around –

bread . . .

Bread has been a basic food since **ancient** times. A Roman **fresco** painted almost two thousand years ago (opposite, far left) shows a bakery, and a clay model (opposite, top right), made five centuries earlier in Greece, shows a woman grinding wheat to make flour.

This Spanish **still life** was painted in the eighteenth century. It shows a very simple meal of bread and figs.

corn . . .

In the early history of America, maize, or corn, was as important as wheat was in Europe. This vase (right), made centuries ago in Peru, is a god with three heads on a body made of corn cobs.

The two girls in this painting (left) are cooking **polenta**, which is a common Italian dish made with cornmeal. The artist is Italian painter Longhi, who lived in the 1700s.

and rice.

In Asian countries such as China and Japan, rice is
a **staple**. These four men, drawn by Japanese artist
Hokusai, are pounding rice into flour for cooking
and baking.

Fish has been
a basic food . . .

This still life of two black-and-white fish was painted by French artist Braque around the middle of the twentieth century.

for a very long time.

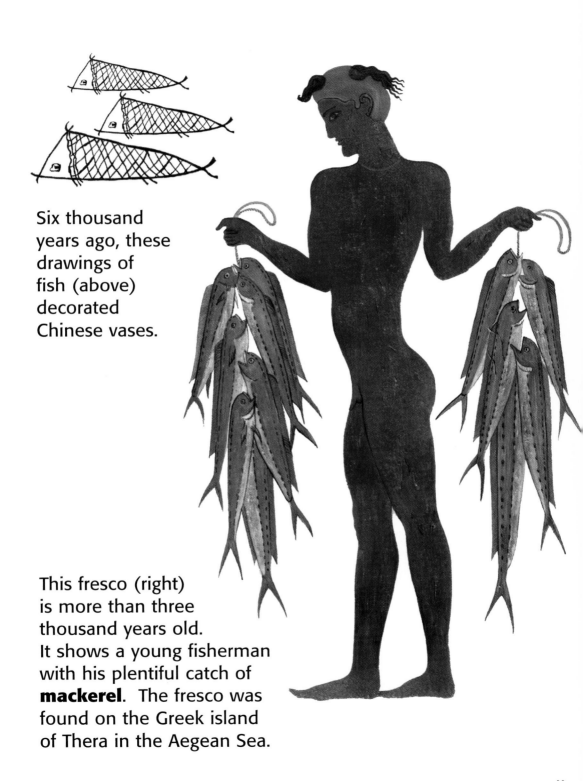

Six thousand
years ago, these
drawings of
fish (above)
decorated
Chinese vases.

This fresco (right)
is more than three
thousand years old.
It shows a young fisherman
with his plentiful catch of
mackerel. The fresco was
found on the Greek island
of Thera in the Aegean Sea.

The same goes for meat.

The beef roast hanging on a cord is a **reproduction** in colored **plaster** by Claes Oldenburg, an American "pop" artist. It was made in 1961.

"Pop" art often **criticized consumerism**, and this hunk of beef doesn't particularly make anyone want to eat meat.

This large painting pictures a well-supplied pantry with meats of all kinds. The painting is a still life of a typical Italian pantry of four centuries ago, when the painting was done.

Milk is a child's first food and . . .

A cow, with her calf tied to one leg, stands patiently as she is being milked in this Egyptian **relief** from nearly four thousand years ago.

In this painting, a cook is pouring milk into a pot. The artist was Jan Vermeer, a great Dutch painter of the 1600s.

is found in every kitchen.

Vegetables and fruits are colorful . . .

Artichokes in a dish were carefully drawn and colored by an Italian artist named Giovanna Garzoni in the seventeenth century. Garzoni loved to paint fruits, vegetables, and flowers.

These six persimmons were painted with very simple lines by Chinese artist Mu Ch'i, more than seven centuries ago. He used ink and brushes, just like those used to write in Chinese.

and healthful foods.

A fruit market...

can be a riot of colors.

This country girl's splendid **array** of fruits and vegetables delights the eye and almost makes your mouth water. Vincenzo Campi, an Italian artist from the sixteenth century, painted the scene, setting it in a landscape instead of at a market.

Soup and desserts are foods that . . .

This can of soup almost looks like a photograph, but it is "pop" art, drawn in the 1960s by American artist Andy Warhol.

This still life of desserts includes cookies and a glass of wine. It was painted about four centuries ago by German artist Georg Flegel.

begin and end a meal.

A variety of foods...

makes a nicely set table.

A nineteenth-century Mexican artist painted this table full of simple country **fare**. The lovely and decorative pottery plates are typical of Mexico.

Food can be arranged on a tray . . .

This dish and its brightly colored assortment of fresh fruits and nuts are all made of **terra-cotta**. It is a sixteenth century piece created in Faenza, an Italian city famous for its pottery, known as Faenze.

and offered to guests – or a goddess.

This tray full of bread, sliced meat, ducks, grapes, figs, and a pomegranate is an offering to the goddess **Isis**. As described in his **tomb** in a colored relief, it was made about 3,300 years ago by an Egyptian **pharaoh**.

People dream of food . . .

Three **portly gents** sleeping under a tree are surrounded by food that is ready to jump into their mouths. Although they look as if they have already stuffed themselves, they continue to dream of things to eat. This scene was painted by Bruegel, a famous Flemish artist, in the mid-sixteenth century.

and eat it even when they are asleep.

GLOSSARY

ancient
relating to a time early in history, from the earliest civilizations until about the time of the Roman Empire

array
a large and attractive or impressive grouping or arrangement of objects

consumerism
the theory that buying more goods improves the economy, or a tendency or need on the part of consumers to buy more and more material goods

contemporary
relating to a person or an event living or happening in current or modern times

criticized
evaluated the good and bad aspects of something or someone, usually focusing more attention on bad points, problems, or faults

expanse
a large area of something, such as water or a landscape, that spreads far and wide without being interrupted by anything unusual or that does not belong

fare
menu, diet, or types of food available for selection

fresco
a painting on a wall; specifically, a type of painting that is typically done on fresh, damp plaster, using water-based paints or coloring

gents
short for gentlemen

horizon
a perceived line that forms a type of boundary, limit, or range to a view of some kind

Isis
the Egyptian goddess of nature

landscape
a wide view of the natural scenery or land forms of a particular area that can be seen all at the same time from one place

mackerel
an important food fish, most commonly found in the northern Atlantic Ocean, that is a member of the tuna family

pharaoh
an ancient Egyptian ruler

plaster
a pastelike combination of materials such as sand and lime, mixed with water, which is commonly spread as a coating onto walls and ceilings, then becomes hard as it dries

polenta
a type of cornmeal mush, made by stewing corn grits in water and served hot with butter, cheese, or cream sauces. In northern Italy, polenta is a staple food, usually served in place of pasta or bread.

"pop" art
a style of modern art in which common, everyday objects, such as hamburgers and soup cans, are the subjects of paintings and sculptures and may even be used as materials for pieces of art

portly
having a thick, bulky, round-shaped body

relief
a form of sculpture in which the details of the figure or design are raised and stick out from or project above a flat surface

reproduction
a duplicate or copy; something made to look exactly like, or very close to, an actual item or object

staple
a substance or material that is a main or basic element or is widely used

still life
a picture or painting, the subject of which is just simple, inanimate objects, such as fruits and flowers, that are not able to move by themselves, usually attractively arranged on a table

terra-cotta
brownish-orange earth, or clay, that hardens when it is baked and is often used to make pottery and roofing tiles

tomb
a chamber or vault, often underground, that is used as a burial place for a corpse (dead person)

PICTURE LIST

pages 4-5 — Erro Gudmundson (20th century): Foodscape, 1964. Stockholm, Modern Museum. Photo Tord Lund/Moderna Museet. © Erro Gudmundson by SIAE, 2000.

page 6 — Fresco of a baker's shop. Roman art, 1st century A.D., from Pompeii. Naples, National Museum. Photo Scala Archives.

Terra-cotta model of a woman grinding wheat. Greek art, 5th century B.C. London, British Museum. Drawing by Fiammetta Dogi.

page 7 — Luis Meléndez (1716-1780): Still Life. Paris, Louvre. Photo Scala Archives.

page 8 — Terra-cotta vessel with a triple divinity wrapped in a bunch of corn cobs. Moche culture, Peru, 300-700 A.D. London, British Museum. Photo Bridgeman/Overseas.

Pietro Longhi (1702-1785): Polenta. Venice, Ca' Rezzonico. Photo Scala Archives.

page 9 — Katsushika Hokusai (1760-1849): Four men trampling rice to make a sweet called "mochi," detail of a drawing. Washington, Freer Gallery of Art. Drawing by Luigi Ieracitano.

page 10 — Georges Braque (1882-1963): Black Fishes, 1942. Paris, Musee National d'Art Moderne. Photo Scala Archives. © Georges Braque by SIAE, 2000.

page 11 — Fish-shaped decorative motif, used on Chinese pottery of the neolithic Yangshao culture, documented in the 5th millennium B.C. Drawing by Luigi Ieracitano.

Fresco showing a fisherman with mackerel. Aegean art, c. 1350 B.C., from Thera. Athens, National Museum. Drawing by Luigi Ieracitano.

page 12 — Claes Oldenburg (b. 1929): Roast Beef, 1961. New York, Sonnabend Gallery. Gallery photo. © Sonnabend Gallery.

pages 12-13 — Jacopo Chimenti (1554-1640): Still Life. Florence, Uffizi. Photo Scala Archives.

page 14 — Milking a cow, relief from an Egyptian sarcophagus, early XI dynasty, 20th century B.C., from Deir el-Bahari. Cairo, Egyptian Museum. Drawing by Luigi Ieracitano.

page 15 — Jan Vermeer (1632-1675): The Cook. Amsterdam, Rijksmuseum. Museum photo.

page 16 — Giovanna Garzoni (1600-1670): Plate of Artichokes. Florence, Galleria Palatina, Pitti Palace. Photo Scala Archives.

page 17 — Mu Ch'i (13th century): Six Persimmons. Kyoto, Ryokoin Temple. Drawing by Luigi Ieracitano.

pages 18-19 — Vincenzo Campi (1536-1591): The Fruit Vender. Milan, Brera. Photo Scala Archives.

page 20 — Andy Warhol (1930-1987): Big Campbell's Soup Can, 19 cents, 1962. Houston, The Menil Collection. Museum photo. © Andy Warhol by SIAE, 2000.

page 21 — Georg Flegel (1566-1638): Still Life with Bread and Sweets. Frankfurt, Staedelsches Kunstinstitut. Photo Joachim Blauel/Artothek.

pages 22-23 – Unknown painter: Country Food, 19th century. Mexico City, National Museum of Art. Museum photo.

page 24 — Plate of fruit in Faenze ceramics. Italian art of the 16th century. Faenza, International Ceramics Museum. Photo Scala Archives.

page 25 — Detail of a fresco showing a plate of offerings. Egyptian art, XIX dynasty, late 14th century B.C. Abydos, Temple of Seti I, Chapel of Isis. Drawing by Luigi Ieracitano.

pages 26-27 — Pieter Bruegel the Elder (1528-1569): Land of Cockaigne. Munich, Alte Pinakothek. Photo Scala Archives.

INDEX